"Wow- great inspirational read. I thought at my age learning to speak another language was out of reach. I'm convinced that I can do it, I will do it, and look forward to succeeding at it" - Ronald P. Scarsdale NY

Finally, a short book that is both practical and fun to read and suited to adults that are serious about becoming fluent in a second language.

Follow the author on his own multi-year long journey as he navigates the road from beginner to fluency.

Packed with easy-to-understand learning techniques, motivation, and sprinkled with nuggets of wisdom and some exciting personal travel stories, this book provides the reader with a clear and achievable roadmap to successfully learn a second language.

Dedication:

To my wonderful family: my daughters, grandkids, son, wife, Mom, Dad, brother, sister, nieces, and nephews. To my grandparents and great grandparents who so many years ago took the ocean voyage from Europe to America in search of a better life. Without them, my amazing life would have never been possible. Thank you all!

Favorite quote:

"You only get one spin in life—so make it count—no regrets"

Table of Contents

CHAPTER 1: INTRODUCTION 5

CHAPTER 2: SET THE GOAL 6

CHAPTER 3: WHY DO YOU WANT TO DO THIS? 8

CHAPTER 4: STRATEGY 9

CHAPTER 5: TACTICS 11

CHAPTER 6: WHAT SHOULD YOU STUDY? 14

CHAPTER 7: THREE "NUGGETS" 17

CHAPTER 8: YOU CAN SUCCEED! 21

CHAPTER 9: MY OWN JOURNEY 22

CHAPTER 10: LITTLE BY LITTLE 24

CHAPTER 11: SIDE BENEFITS 26

CHAPTER 12: REALITY 28

CHAPTER 14: SELF-IMPROVEMENT 34

CHAPTER 15: SECOND TIME IS A CHARM 38

CHAPTER 16: TRAVEL THERE AND GET PLUGGED IN 41

CHAPTER 17: THE LEARNING REALLY BEGINS 44

CHAPTER 18: THE LEARNING GROWS 47

CHAPTER 19: THE FOG STARTS LIFTING 50

CHAPTER 20: CLOSE BUT NO CIGAR 54

CHAPTER 21: THE LAST SUPPER 55

CHAPTER 22: A LIGHTBULB GOES OFF 58

CHAPTER 23: NEXT LEVEL MOVE 60

CHAPTER 24: CONQUERING SELF-DOUBT 62

CHAPTER 25: TORNIAMO A ROMA! 65

CHAPTER 26- "THE OBSTACLE IS THE WAY" 67

CHAPTER 27: BACK TO BASICS 68

CHAPTER 28: BEYOND LANGUAGE 72

CHAPTER 29: LOCKDOWN 74

CHAPTER 30: THE LIGHT AT THE END OF THE TUNNEL IS NOW VISIBLE 75

CHAPTER 31: ONWARD AND UPWARD! 83

CHAPTER 32: CONCLUSION AND SUCCESS 87

Chapter 1: Introduction

My grandfather used to tell me, "Nothing worthwhile comes easy. "

And he was so right. Without any doubt, I can tell you, that in order to achieve success in any life endeavor, it always takes a plan; hard work; frustrations and failures; trial and error; patience; pushing yourself past your normal comfort zones and into new, uncomfortable, uncharted situations; and an emotional and burning desire to reach the finish line, as well as the flexibility to adapt and change as you move forward toward your goal. I've also learned to "start at the end." In other words, I try to imagine how what I'm thinking about doing will look like when it's done. Kind of like the saying, "Before you get into it, think about what will come out of it."

And my mom would famously say, "Be careful what you wish for because it may just come true."

How right they both were!

Chapter 2: Set the Goal

It doesn't matter what language you have in mind. It could be English, French, Portuguese, Chinese, Russian, German, Japanese, Hebrew, Arabic—any language. If you read this short book, become inspired, and get to work learning that second language, you can succeed in becoming bilingual. I chose Italian. My first language is English. My language-learning journey took about five years. Yours may be shorter or longer, but it can become a reality for you. It may even be one of or the most satisfying accomplishment of your life. That's how I feel about it now. Academically, it was the toughest, yet most rewarding thing I have ever done.

It is an asset that I did not have a few years ago but possess now and will still have to the day I die. Someday (I hope) when I'm old, I can look back on this journey, and subsequent accomplishment, and be proud. Also, hopefully, this short book will serve as an inspiration and a roadmap for hundreds or thousands or hundreds of thousands, of people all around the world, who are able to do the same thing. This would be so rewarding and positive for everyone, myself included! My target audience includes people like myself—adults mainly, but I imagine it would also work for kids and teens. This short book is geared more toward adults (past school years) who possess the time, the motivation, and the self-discipline to be serious and committed to taking a language journey. This short book represents my best and most honest attempt to distill my own language-learning journey for you in a way that can become your language-learning journey.

Chapter 3: Why Do You Want to Do This?

I believe that before you begin this journey the most important question that you must wrestle with and answer is why. Why do you want to learn a second language? Is this something that you must do for economic reasons, like maybe you have a better job opportunity in another country? Or you and your family are emigrating to a new country for other reasons? Or maybe your current job allows for a promotion for bilingual employees? Or possibly, like me, it's just something that you want to do, feel the time is right for, or have something to prove to yourself or others, you flick the switch and do it. If you don't have a compelling why, then your chances of success will be low. If you do have a strong why, where it absolutely must happen, and you feel deep inside yourself that it will happen, then your chances of success will be quite good. Remember, you are the one in control of this. It's you who drives the train—no one else. If you are able to ultimately succeed in becoming fluent in a second language, then you are responsible for the success. If you ultimately fail or quit or procrastinate, then you are responsible for the failure. You should have a serious and honest conversation with yourself regarding your motivations, your reasons, to learn a second language. This, I believe, is the first crucial step forward in your journey.

Chapter 4: Strategy

You must feel a strong connection, a deep and emotional connection, to this new language you plan to learn. Without it, don't waste the time and energy. You will not make it to the finish line. There are just too many hurdles, too many obstacles, too many brick walls, too many distractions, too many interruptions, and too much time you will need to succeed. It requires this emotional connection to push you forward, give you the strength and energy to get past all of these obstacles. Plus, the strong emotional connection will be instrumental in helping you develop the daily study habits that you must acquire in order accomplish your mission.

Also mandatory for success is a strong commitment to see it through to the end until you become fluent in that new language. Not a general commitment like ""I'll get into "shape" or '" I'll make more money this year." These types of commitments are too vague, too weak, too commonly started and failed. Like so many past New Year's resolutions that lasted for a week or a month and then just faded away. Success here requires a specific commitment. I will become fluent in this new language in a few years, and I'm committed to do whatever it takes to get me there." It requires a commitment level probably as strong as anything you have ever done, or maybe even a bit more than that. For myself, the language journey I took was the most committed, focused, and mentally challenging thing I've ever seen through in my life. This is a journey with basically no days off. It must become an everyday thing, a part of your daily life. This language-learning journey must be your new habit.

Chapter 5: Tactics

I've discovered along the way that it's more about persistence than talent. You don't have to be a genius. You just have to want it—really bad. You must study and practice this new language every day, for about an hour, so it becomes a daily habit. If somehow you miss a day (it's happened to me, but rarely), simply increase your study time to offset the loss until it's even again. Don't get upset or frustrated or lose focus on your main goal. Every once in a while, life gets in the way and screws up our schedules. It's ok, but don't allow this to become a regular thing. I'm talking maybe one day every few months, but that's it. I say this because I have learned in life just how easy it is to break a routine with just a few missed days. You cannot allow that to happen to you if you are truly serious and committed to your language journey.

You may want to announce to your friends or your family that you are doing this. For some people it may help because they don't want to fail and have to explain why. That in itself could be enough motivation to succeed. Others, like me, decide to keep it to themselves and make it a game between the language and me, sort of a secret and a little fun. No doubt the people very close to me watched me slink away at different times of the day and night, could probably overhear parts of the lessons, and obviously knew what I was doing. But to anyone outside my closest family, my language journey was not known.

Then the day came, when I had already reached the goal, and we were somewhere together, usually a restaurant, or a social event, and they would watch me speak in fluent Italian to a server or another patron or the restaurant owner or a friend from Italy.

Most would say afterward, "I didn't know you actually spoke Italian. "

My nonchalant answer is usually, "Yes, I taught myself over the last few years "

My goal is to always try to be humble, a trait my Grandpa Joe would often remind me as a young person would serve me well in life. As tempting as it may be to cast myself as some kind aristocratic genius, man of the world, conqueror of knowledge, it suits me just fine to say "Yes, I do" and nothing more. If I'm pushed as to how I was able to learn this language, then I respond by saying "lots of practice" and just leave it at that. I saved the details, I saved emotions, I saved the "" recipe" for this short book. It's been building up inside of me for months. I am so proud of myself, I'm so happy I was able to cross the finish line of fluency and have a roadmap that really worked. My goal is to help you get there, too. That would give me even more pride, more happiness, more warmth, knowing others, especially adults, are fulfilling their language goals with my help. And I could just imagine that when new and different minds set out on this language journey, how many different approaches, techniques, systems, and content could prove better, faster, and go steps further than my journey. It could be great if readers and doers find a platform to collaborate with each other, to inspire and motivate each other, to improve the language learning "" recipe" even more.

At the end of this book, we can communicate via email. We can set up a blog, a website, do an occasional podcast or zoom call to personalize the experience, share techniques, help one another, and maybe start a language learning community for adults that really works. Maybe some language contests or competitions would be fun and helpful. Let's see if we can build something new together, ok?

***Writer's note:** Over my five plus year language journey, I spent a copious amount of time searching over the Internet for better language learning solutions. Lots of books claiming, "Learn Italian in five minutes a day" and similar "" shortcut" catchy titles, blogs, and podcasts that all turned out to have a sales pitch at the end and were simply looking for your credit card info. Some helpful language apps (like Duolingo) that really did help, and many books that were mainly short stories or workbooks, many I bought and used, some good, some not. So, to end this writer's note, I can say with certainty that in order to become fluent in a second language, as an adult, there are no" quick fixes"! No shortcuts. No magic pills. It's only about working hard, working smart, staying committed and connected, and seeing it all the way through to success.*

Whether your motivation to become bilingual is economic or personal, it must be not just strong, but one of, if not *the* single most important priorities in your life.

Chapter 6: What Should You Study?

Your learning journey—what you study, when you study, how long you study—is totally up to you. You want it to be fun, diverse, and exciting so you don't get bored and quit. So, do what I did and" mix it" up:" journals, workbooks, verb and conjugation charts, read blogs, and watch YouTube videos and vlogs in that language, watch movies, short stories, newspapers, TV shows, download music, hang out with native speakers, develop relationships with native speakers, and travel when possible as much as possible. And make time, every day, to do one or two or three of these things for at least an hour. You will find some "comfort" spots" where you are able to be most productive.

In my first year of self-studying, I typically reached my daily "study time" limit" at about forty-five minutes. By year two, I was up to an hour a day. In years three and four, I felt comfortable at about ninety total minutes per day of various studying. By year five (I'm currently at five and a half years), I've jacked up my daily "Italian" time" to about two hours, and during the pandemic lockdown months, was hitting three hours a day regularly. When you do it daily in small pieces, mixing in lots of different things, it's easy, it doesn't feel like work, and I honestly look forward to my next little lesson.

For example, each morning now when I wake up and enjoy a cup of coffee, I sit at my desk in my home office, and do a ten-minute Duolingo app lesson. After showering and leaving for work, I stop at a bagel shop, sit by myself at a small table. While eating, I will read about fifteen minutes of *Gazzetta di Parma* in that app. (It's an Italian language newspaper from one of my favorite cities.) And while driving, if I'm not playing word and phrase games in my head, by myself, then I'm listening to either Italian language music or an Italian language news station on the car radio. Even though I'm on the phone a lot or thinking about my construction projects, I probably absorb fifteen to twenty minutes of language from word games and another fifteen to twenty minutes from the radio daily.

Then during the late morning, on WhatsApp, I'll call or text my friend and business partner in Rome, usually lasting ten to fifteen minutes. Later in the day, when I stop at my real office, I always find another ten minutes for a second Duolingo app lesson. Upon arriving home in the early evening with a glass of wine before dinner, at my desk again, I knock out my third Duolingo app lesson of the day. Finally, after dinner, I usually read fifteen to twenty minutes of an Italian language book, on some subject that I enjoy. Then, when retiring into bed, instead of watching news or some silly show, I pop in a DVD of an Italian language movie (which I have over a hundred) and watch fifteen or twenty minutes, or more, on Netflix or Prime Video or stream an Italian TV series or movie.

So, all said, on a typical day (living in South Florida), I absorb approximately two hours, maybe a bit more, of various forms of Italian language. I've developed my comfort spots, comfort times, and comfort content that has become a habit I repeat day in and day out. This routine has evolved over time and it works and it's fun and I enjoy it. You can find your own content, your own spots to study, your own word games, and make time during your day. I believe the key is to keep it interesting, stay connected, and make it a daily habit. I really believe it's that simple. Maybe you have a habit now, like watching hours of TV every night or knocking down a few pints with your pals at the pub every night or surfing the Web or social media an hour or two each day. By the way, none of those activities are productive or will grow your value as a person. So, think about replacing one of the time-wasting, dead-end habits with a new, productive, mind growing habit like learning a second language? Could be just what you need!

Chapter 7: Three "Nuggets"

Recently, three nuggets of wisdom have crossed my path that are worth sharing. The first came out of a travel magazine and hit me like a ton of bricks when I read it. It's about how "you only get one spin," meaning you only go around once in life, so make it count! The clock keeps ticking. Days, weeks, months, years fly by. We get numb from the comfort of routine as life begins to slip by. But fear not. You can embrace a new adventure. You can grab it with both hands and squeeze it tight. You can rise above your routine, your monotony, get comfortable being uncomfortable, trying something new and hard and feeling some pain. And the reward for the discomfort of your new adventure will be a better, richer, fuller life. Before you die, make sure that you really lived. You only get one spin!

The second nugget was brought forward in a podcast I watched by a man everyone is familiar with, the greatest bodybuilder of all time, the former Governor of California, the actor, Arnold Schwarzenegger. Without any doubt a man who embodies the American dream with fame, fortune, accomplishment and apparent happiness. In fact, my fourteen-year-old son, Vinny, has Arnold's poster on the wall in our home gym, as inspiration during his daily pump routines. In this short podcast, Arnold lays out what he considers the four main components to his success. First, he says it begins with a vision of who or what you want to be. It must be clearly defined, with a plan to get there and driven by not just a strong, but an almost fanatical work ethic. Second, he says not to listen to the naysayers, just tune them out and keep forging ahead. What do they know anyway? Third, he insists that you should not get discouraged, but instead double down, or triple down, on your training. Have patience, because it takes time to get there. Remember, Rome wasn't built in a day! And fourth, he talks about how your new skill set will be an asset, something you will always have, something that will make you more valuable than the next guy.

He finishes the podcast by sharing the findings of a recently completed, comprehensive survey conducted throughout Europe, Canada, and the USA. It found that about three-fourths of everyone surveyed are miserable with either their job, their lives, and where they fit into society. Only about a quarter of the respondents reported being happy. Hard to believe but true. The vast majority of people are in jobs they hate, lives they feel are incomplete, and feel apart from the society that they live in. Arnold points to this seventy-five percent as people who lack clear visions and simply "float" through life without plans, having no real destinations to arrive at. He then highlights the "happy" twenty-five percent and describes what they have in common is vision linked to a plan with the willingness to work hard to achieve that vision, the ability to ignore the pessimists, the patience and determination to continue forward, and an almost religious belief that you will become something special.

He ends with this question to the audience. "Do you want to be in the miserable seventy-five percent or the happy twenty-five percent? It's your choice".

So, it is my belief that by simply learning to speak a second language will become one of the hardest, one of the most fun, one of the most valuable, and one of the most self-rewarding things you ever accomplish in your life. Not a bad reason, agreed?

The third nugget jumped out of my TV screen the other day while watching a short business show interview with the legendary value investor, the "Sage of Omaha," Warren Buffett. While answering a question put to him regarding what he believes makes him such a successful investor, he responded with one simple word: patience. He went on to explain how Father Time is your friend and how instant gratification is a mere illusion. He believes the only way to achieve real results, lasting results, is to think long term and have patience. He explains how success comes only as a result of the long and grinding journey and that the payoff includes not just reaching a specific goal, but also a strong feeling of inner satisfaction that very few people are lucky enough to feel. He explains in detail that in order to possess the necessary patience to see your journey to a successful end, you will need a big dose of self-discipline coupled with a smart system that you consistently work overtime. He adds that while it's good to always have your eye on the big prize (in your case fluency), it's even more important to focus on your daily systems, the daily lessons, the repeated habits and actions that you take day in and day out, over and over. This is how you get closer and closer and finally reach that goal!

I believe that I have learned, through over fifty years of living, some fundamental truths that I want to share with you, in the hope that you can use some of them to improve your own lives, be more successful, be prouder, be happier, be more productive, be more special, and, of course, succeed in learning a second language.

Chapter 8: You Can Succeed!

In this book, my first writing project, my goal is to show you how you can, as an adult (young or old), become fluent in a second language. No school, no classes, no fancy tutors. You can teach yourself. When you decide to commit to the end goal (fluency), then you will form a new habit, the habit of practicing and learning a little more in that language, every single day until it's done. It must become one of your main life priorities—ahead of watching TV, ahead of resting, ahead of socializing, ahead of surfing the Internet and social media. In order to be successful in this language journey, you will need to recalibrate your mind a bit, view this as an adventure, something fun and enjoyable. Occasionally, think about the finished product, the end result, you speaking a second language fluently—how nice that will be and how good it will make you feel. The satisfaction it will give you. This view will keep you motivated. And if it's fun, and it's interesting and you will want to do it even more. Also, you will need to use your free time better, like when you are driving or commuting, during "alone" meals, at night before bedtime, finding yourself early for a meeting, or just about any piece of time during the day where you can take a few minutes or longer, whip out your verb book, open your language app, pop in a CD, something that adds to your language growth, and focus on the new language. All these little bits and pieces of extra daily learning will add up to a substantial body of language knowledge over time. It will pay off, and it's a good, healthy habit!

Chapter 9: My Own Journey

I'll take you on my journey (actually several fits and starts) where I finally got serious, made a commitment to myself, felt a strong connection to the Italian language, pushed forward with the work of learning, utilizing journals, books, apps, CDs, group lessons, native speaking friends and relatives, and movies. After a period of about five years, I can proudly consider myself conversational and basically fluent in Italian.

Honestly, I'm more than just proud of this accomplishment. First, having several native Italian friends and vacationing in Italy several times a year, my ability to understand and speak Italian have made things better and easier for me. Secondly, I have developed several business relationships between here and Italy that have blossomed into profitable ventures, and finally, I've once again proven to myself that when I commit to something, I can accomplish it, and that feels really good inside!

Before you choose to commit to your own second language journey, please consider the following very seriously: success will not be in a week, a month, or even a year. Success will be several years out. So, if you are an instant gratification type person, don't even try. You must study and practice every day, literally, because unless you are absolutely and totally committed to spend anywhere from fifteen minutes to an hour and eventually even more every single day learning and practicing just a little more, - you will wind up missing days, breaking the habit, and ultimately failing. You also must approach the learning process from multiple angles—verb and study guides, your own notes or journals, reading newspapers and short stories in that language, watching movies in that language, keeping learning apps like Duolingo on your phone and moving through them daily, creating your own word and phrase games, getting friendly with some native speakers and practice your words and phrases and listening skills, try some CDs or audiobooks that you can listen to while driving, and if economically possible, go to that country as frequently as possible and immerse yourself in the language.

Keep it interesting, keep it fun, and mix it up regularly to avoid boredom or monotony. It's important to really look forward to your next lesson by embracing it and enjoying it. I currently subscribe to *Gazzetta di Parma*, a daily online newspaper in one of my favorite towns in Italy. Each day, even for just five or ten minutes, I open this app and read up on a story or two, a new restaurant review, or some political drama unfolding in Parma. It transports me for a few minutes to a place I love and care about and so look forward to revisiting shortly. It helps keep my connection strong. If I encounter a word, or phrase, that is unfamiliar, I move over to my dictionary app and look it up. I firmly believe that only with daily practice over a multiyear period utilizing many forms of learning and immersion formats that you will be successful at speaking and understanding your second language.

Chapter 10: Little by Little

I think a good comparison could be training to compete in a twenty-six-mile marathon run. Let's say you're forty years old and have not done any serious exercise in over twenty years. (Note: at age forty, I decided it was time to "get back in "shape," and I followed this exact plan, never with marathon aspirations, but my end goal was to achieve five miles, quit smoking, and in doing so get into reasonable physical shape. This journey took the better part of one year, and I did succeed, but have since run on and off as my priorities have changed.) At this moment, you would be lucky to run even one mile. If you devoted some time, each and every day to running and eating and sleeping properly, then after about a year you should be able to go about five miles without passing out. From there, you could add various training techniques to your daily runs (weight vest, hills, sprints, altitude, nutritional supplements) and add maybe five miles per year to your maximum run distance, achieving the goal of twenty-six miles after five years of dedication and daily training. Imagine what great physical shape you would be in at that point. Imagine the feeling of knowing that you set out to accomplish something that seemed so difficult and so far off, and that you made it, you did it, that plaque is hanging on your wall for all to see that you completed the twenty-six-mile marathon. How many people said you were crazy, you were wasting your time, that you could never do it? Most of them were talkers and not doers, stuck in their own mediocre lives doing the bare minimum to "get by" and never aspiring to accomplish something hard, something new, something great. Remember, you only get one spin!

In this short book, I will show you what worked, what didn't, and hopefully provide you with a clear road map, or recipe, for you to achieve success in speaking a second language

Chapter 11: Side benefits

In case you didn't know, speaking a second language opens your world up to so many new and beautiful things—things like literature, music, food, wine, movies, art, and friendships, you can now understand things that you had no idea even existed! My point is that the time and effort you invest in the learning process is paid back to you one hundred times over in the succeeding phase. Yes, it's some hard work; yes, it takes a few years; and yes, you will have to make some sacrifices, but yes, it's worth it every bit. Speaking a second language will put you in an exclusive club of exceptional people, give you a deep and warm feeling of personal satisfaction and accomplishment, and stretch your brain to a new limit like it's never been stretched before. I promise you the mental gymnastics "you will perform during the learning process will sharpen your mind and spill over to other areas of your life. I can tell you with one hundred percent certainty that my ability to remember details, numbers, dates, and think clearer and faster and smarter are the byproducts of my language learning journey. I am a home builder by trade, and today make fewer mistakes, better decisions, smarter plans, and lots more money than I did five years ago.

Just recently, I was standing in line at Home Depot to pay for some tools. A much older man in front of me was trying to communicate with the cashier to return an item, but after several minutes was having no success. As I listened to him, he was speaking Italian and trying to bend it into English, with both him and the cashier getting frustrated and nowhere.

So, I got the man's attention with a *"parli Italiano?"*

He responded, *"Si, sono di Italia, sto provando a ritornare questa macchina, ma non ho il scontrino"*.

Basically, he was trying to return a power tool and did not have his receipt. I explained to him in Italian that the store policy is to give a store credit, not a cash refund if the receipt is not presented. He agreed, the cashier issued him the credit, and his problem was solved. This little encounter also made me feel good. Not only was I able to help this old guy, but also in the confidence and ease of my ability to just dive in and speak Italian. It occurred to me that I'm really good at speaking this language. All that hard work has paid off!

Chapter 12: Reality

Not so fun fact: As most people get older, they not only get further away from their "study years"," they tend to watch more TV, use their brains less, have less patience, and these factors make it ever more difficult to learn a new language. But do not despair. It can be done! I did it. I'm not a genius. What I am is motivated, determined, connected, and consistent. I developed new habits, study habits, that are part of my daily routine, every day without fail. Some days it may be only thirty minutes, other days it could be an hour or even two hours, or more, depending on the activity, my work schedule, my mood, my energy level, my motivation that particular day. Regardless, each and every day, for more than five years now, including today, I learn a little bit more, I practice a little bit more, I get just a little bit better at speaking Italian. The language lessons for me have become part of my daily routine, like brushing my teeth, like taking a shower, and like eating breakfast.

These are habits that you will need to develop in order to succeed. I believe to follow the language journey all the way to fluency, you will need something that burns strong inside you, maybe something you feel that you need to prove to yourself or to someone else. Maybe just a love of that particular language or culture is enough motivation for you. Some emotional connection. Maybe some empty hole that you need to fill. Something that will make you more complete. Something that will give you a sense of personal accomplishment. We weren't all academic superstars in our youth, but now we can show ourselves and others that we are somehow smart, educated, accomplished, and bilingual.

Chapter 13: My First Try

Fits and Starts:

I remember as a child, growing up in a middle-class suburban neighborhood to English-speaking parents and grandparents, attending public schools, and taking the standard Spanish and French classes. How I used to think how cool it would be to actually speak another language fluently, effortlessly, like a native. How it would also make me a more valuable person as I grew older and entered the workforce. That there could be some special job or special mission for someone with my bilingual skills. However, I had no personal, familial, or even emotional connection to either Spanish or French. Plus, this was middle school and high school where my priorities were simply graduating and moving ahead to college, playing ice hockey and golf, lifting weights and, of course, girls. Being fluent in a second language was way down on the priority list, more of a vague wish than a serious goal. Kind of like "I wish I lived in that big house," or "I wish I drove that fancy car," or "I wish I had muscles like that guy."

However, this dream of being bilingual seemed to always be in the back of my mind, sometimes creeping forward to conscious thoughts but never really taking shape or feeling any burning desire to explore further. This stayed in the back of my mind for many years. Maybe it just had to be the right time in my life.

False start:

It happened when I was around forty-two years old. I had been recently divorced and had become seriously involved with a woman who was originally from Colombia and, of course, spoke fluent Spanish. I thought to impress her more, I could learn to speak Spanish, so I went ahead, purchased a few "learning guides" and CDs at Barnes & Noble, and began practicing. Not easy. Spanish, like Italian or any of the romance languages, has masculine and feminine rules; past, present, future and all the associated conjugation rules; and many hundreds of verbs to learn, plus many nuances and exceptions and irregulars. It became clear this was no simple task. So it's not going to be easy. No problem. I'll think out of the box a bit, and it should come to me eventually.

Over the next few years, we made about a dozen trips to Colombia. And always in the weeks leading up before each trip I would double down on the study guides, create my own travel journal for verbs and commonly used phrases, and devote time each day, even during the trip, to updating my journal and practice phrases. I thought I was doing pretty good, but for some reason my ability to understand when others were speaking Spanish and my ability to speak Spanish were frustratingly bad.

I recall reflecting back on this low point in my Spanish journey, and only when I was really honest with myself. Honest in the fact that first I really did not "feel the love" for the language, like it just wasn't part of me; and second, although I had done quite a bit of studying and practicing over the past three or four years, I often felt bored and was easily distracted during my almost daily sessions; and third, for whatever reason, I just didn't want it badly enough. I didn't need to make it happen. I just didn't have the burning desire to be a Spanish speaker.

So, trying to impress my then girlfriend (by the way we got married and have four beautiful children) was just not enough to get me to the promised land. One day, I took that pile of study guides, journals, books, and CD's, threw them in the garbage, and promised myself someday, soon, I would learn another language, just not Spanish.

For the record, I enjoy hearing Spanish spoken, one of my favorite singers is Marco Antonio Solis, who sings all of his beautiful songs in Spanish. My wife and kids all speak Spanish. I am a history buff and have read dozens of books on the Central and South American journeys through the ages. One of my heroes is Simon Bolivar, and I love Spanish food. So I have absolutely nothing against Spanish, but for some reason it was a language I just couldn't embrace deeply enough to become proficient.

Looking back on this "Spanish "chapter of my language journey, although I fell short of my original goal (to understand and speak fluent Spanish), it was the first time in my life that I made an honest, sustained effort to learn a new language. In addition, I built up some decent study habits, and created my own verb journals that would help me in my next language adventure, *Italiano*. This failed attempt to learn Spanish was not a total loss or waste of time. I believe that this was, at least for me, a necessary step in my language evolution process. Let me explain in this small diversion from language learning.

Chapter 14: Self-improvement

I come from a pretty big family, and all of my siblings are college graduates and professionals in different fields. Unfortunately, although I graduated high school, I was a college dropout.

I worked some tough jobs in some tough fields. And as a result, my path toward knowledge and business success has been both long and hard, at least when compared to my siblings, who quickly and seemingly easily moved up the professional ladder. So, I think I always had a chip on my shoulder, felt I had to work harder and embraced risk and challenges as I moved through adulthood. There was always a feeling in the back of my mind that I had to prove to everyone that yes, I am smart also; and yes, I can be just as successful, or even more so. And at the same time, I never had any fears, never considered failure, never thought for even a minute that I would fall short. I would make it and make it big. Not too big, but big enough to satisfy my dreams. To give my family everything they needed. To be proud of who I was and that my journey, although still in progress, has reached and surpassed most of my original goals.

My best friend was always my own sense of confidence in myself. I knew from a young age that I would never let myself down. I trust myself. I believe in my ability to make things happen. There have been many times in my life, that I have come to major crossroads, where a serious decision had to be made, a certain "scary" thing had to be done, a major life event was ready to happen. It was really "Go" time. And looking back on everything, now in my late fifties, looking back on the last twenty-five years at least, I can say with honesty and accuracy that most of my decisions were good, logical, productive, fair, courageous, and resulted in my life trajectory moving steadily in the up direction. But this was no accident. I think that at around the age of thirty, in the midst of both personal and business frustrations, I was able to be honest with myself about how I was living, but even more important I was able to analyze my decision-making process, and thus discovered a fatal flaw that ran through many of my life choices. The flaw turned out to be my making big decisions (career, relationship, risky behavior) too quickly without critical analysis, without real thought, without a process. I was literally able to link the three worst life mistakes I had made with this flaw. I remember the moment like a light was switched on, like it was just yesterday. This was probably the most important moment of my life. This was my turning point. I was now able to look ahead, see my future, and be excited about it!

I recall spending weeks, months, reading about systems to help me make better decisions. I discovered a specific technique—I believe it's called the "Ben Franklin"—that seemed to work the best for me, and I still use it to this day. It's become a habit. It's really simple, and here is how it goes. When facing a major life decision (not what shirt to wear today, not what to eat for lunch today, we're talking about things that will impact your life for months or years to come), simply sit down at your desk, with peace and quiet and privacy, take out a sheet of blank paper, draw a line down the middle, on one side write down all the pros, and on the other side write down all of the cons of the results that will occur from the decision you are considering. Think hard, be accurate, and complete both sides, but refrain from making the decision that day. It's important to remember not to discuss this with others, don't ask opinions, etc. You alone have more than enough intelligence to make a good decision. Understand that other people, even ones who may love you, have their own agendas, and that will often result in bad advice, even if they don't mean you any harm. Don't rush it. Don't let anyone try to pressure you. It could be a few days, or even a few weeks, but by revisiting the pro versus con sheet, giving it serious, critical, rational thought. Even doing more due diligence on the issue at hand will ultimately lead you to the right decision.

The old phrase "I'm going to sleep on it" is actually a really good strategy. Teamed up with the Ben Franklin approach, I have identified many decisions and solutions to serious problems that just "came to me" as I was waking up. I can't really explain it. Maybe it's that the subconscious mind is able to better sort out all of the pros and cons when relaxed. Maybe during our busy and stress-filled days our brains find it hard to focus properly on important issues that require strategic analysis. Maybe our brains work better while we sleep. Analyze the facts, listen to your gut, let it "marinate" for a while, or sleep on it for a few nights, then make your decision. I promise you will be happier, healthier, and wealthier if you follow this path. It works for me, and it will work for you!

In addition to the Ben Franklin and the "sleep on it" techniques, there was something else, maybe even more effective at solving problems and making better decisions—my mom. Without sounding too mushy, my mom has always been my biggest cheerleader. Since childhood, my mom would always assure me that I was smart, I was capable, and if I put my mind to it, could accomplish just about anything. During my younger adulthood, it was my Mom who would call me out on bad behavior or bad decisions. She would tell me I had limitless potential and could be doing so much better. These words hit me hard, hurt more than a punch in the face, but looking back they were a necessary medicine that was needed at the time.

Thank you, Mom. I wouldn't be who I am today, or where I am today, without your encouragement, your belief in me, your love (sometimes tough but just what the doctor ordered).

Chapter 15: Second Time Is a Charm

Il viaggio in lingua Italiana (the Italian language journey):

In case I haven't mentioned, my mom is a Calabrese. Her family is from Calabria, a region in southern Italy. Her father, my Grandpa Joe, who passed away in 1985, had been a strong influence on me in my younger days. Although he could speak and understand Italian, as his parents were 'off the boat', he chose, like most Italian Americans of his day, to almost always speak English and speak it well. It was very important to his generation to assimilate and become "real" Americans. They were proud to be here, worked hard, followed the rules, and mainly succeeded by building families and businesses that continue to this day. My Grandpa Joe was also a great cook. He taught me many important lessons in life, but that in itself could be an entire book, maybe even a series of books!

So, I imagine my Italian language journey started way back, unbeknownst to me at that time, listening from another room as my Grandpa would speak to my Grandma in Italian, wishing I could understand what they were saying. I also have vivid memories of watching that scene in the restaurant where Michael and *Sollozzo* were speaking Italian during the meal, before the shooting in *The Godfather* movie when it was released in the early seventies. There were a few words that I could understand, but mostly it was a mystery, but a mystery I needed to solve someday. That restaurant was on Gun Hill Road in the Bronx, New York, my Grandpa's neighborhood. I've eaten there many times, and I could feel a connection to all of it: the movie, the food, the culture, the conversation. But at that age, I was not yet ready to embrace the work required to speak and understand Italian.

Looking back, I think the seed was planted in me around this time, but the soil and the weather were not aligned properly to allow that seed to grow, although some roots were set deep inside and those roots would one day, when the time was right, branch out and grow into a tree.

Wish to plan to jump-off point: A little over five years ago, soon after all the Colombia trips and my capitulation with the Spanish language, we took our first family vacation to Italy. It was a kind of spur of the moment plan. We live in Palm Beach, Florida, and were approaching our middle daughter's sweet sixteen party, where most of our relatives and friends were planning on flying into town for the big bash. Then one of our nieces was also having her sweet sixteen party, in New York, just a few days later. We had a family meeting and agreed that following the New York bash for our niece, we would fly directly to Milan, Italy, rent a car, and spend a few weeks traveling around the north and central cities of Italy. Why not? Things were good, the kids had summer vacation, and my wife and myself had reached a point in our business lives where we could take time away, travel in style, and not have to worry. In the month leading up to the big bashes and big trip, we did the research, booked all the flights, the hotels, some special events, and were pretty well prepared for the "big month." In fact, I started to think long and hard about a few trips to

Italy I had made as a child with my family. I could remember the Roman Coliseum, the David statue in Florence, snowy roads as we crossed the Alps into Switzerland one Christmas, the smells, the tastes, the sounds. My dad driving for hours on end from this city to that city. Us kids smooshed into the back of a little Fiat. All these memories that had been bottled up for so long came rushing back at once. As the start date approached, I became more and more excited, almost like a tingling feeling, a feeling I had felt only a few times in my life.

Chapter 16: Travel There and Get Plugged in

Fast forward past the two sweet sixteen parties, we flew to Milan, picked up our Alfa Romeo car rental at the airport, programed the GPS, and headed south toward our first city, Cinque Terre, a beautiful and ancient cluster of small towns cut into a mountainside at the edge of the sea. After a few days of sightseeing, great seafood, amazing wines, and lots of walking and hiking, we headed east and checked into our second city, Florence.

Florence, or Firenze to Italians, is a most incredible city. Full of art, architecture, scooters, fashion, foods, beautiful people, and lots of tourists, Firenze is unique and beautiful and romantic and so much more. We arrived in the early evening, around dinner time. The moment I stepped outside of our car and took a deep breath, able to smell all the wonderful smells of baking and cooking and stone and wood and Florentine air, I was hit by a rush, like I had stepped into a time machine and had been transported back over forty years to the last time I had been in Florence, at around age ten. It was the same smells, the same sounds, the same winds, the same everything! Except, of course, I'm no longer ten years old, and standing beside me are my wife and a batch of teenage children, not my mom and dad and brother and sister. This was a very happy and emotional moment in my life. I had returned to a place that I always considered so special, so magical. All the memories that were overwhelming me with emotions were good, warm, and I felt so content to be back in Florence, after so long.

I recall also thinking about some unfinished business, two things in particular. First, I recalled an ice cream called a *Riccio,* that I had seen as a child in so many shop windows, only to be told that since it was winter, it was not available. I had vowed to myself as a 10-year-old that someday I would return to Florence and have a Riccio. Well, as it turns out, *Riccio* is not a brand, it just means rich in Italian. Basically, back then, before the gelato craze, all ice creams were essentially a *Riccio*. So that dream wasn't going to happen. Oh well.

Second, I remember my long ago wish to learn to speak Italian, not as a bumbling tourist with a few "where is the bathroom or how do I get to" phrases, but to speak it like a native with confidence, with pride. I wanted the ability to converse with people, understand what they were saying, and be able to tell them what I needed to say. Not freeze up, not whip out my phone and go to Google Translate, not try to twist my English words into Italian words. This short stay in Florence, a little over five years ago, was the moment that my Italian language learning journey really started. I purchased an empty, leather bound journal book, maybe one hundred pages total, kept it by my side during the entire trip. Each day, I would write down various words and phrases that seemed important. At restaurants, at stores, at hotels, I would ask the staff to explain and translate certain foods, courses, equipment, anything that was visible. I would take notes in my journal, even draw a basic picture of an object, with the Italian word or phrase next to it. This helped me, in the beginning, to match a visual object to a specific word. Writing and drawing pictures is quite easy.

Listening to Italian people speak Italian to each other and trying to understand what they are actually saying at this very early stage in my learning journey was both difficult and frustrating. I wanted so badly to speak, to understand, to communicate, but did not yet possess the knowledge or the tools to make it happen. I picked up a few dozen words and maybe a dozen phrases that I could actually remember and use during this first trip. I recall on the return flight home reviewing my journal, which was nearly full, and promising myself that as soon as I made it home, I would work on creating a study plan for myself, and a plan to return to beautiful Italy in no less than six months, in order to both experience new cities and adventures and to advance my language-learning experience.

Chapter 17: The Learning Really Begins

My first day home in Florida, I called my friend Marianna. Born and raised in Rome, Marianna was a language teacher at a local college, spoke fluent Italian, and was a close friend of our family. After telling her all about the big Italy trip, I asked her advice as to the best way to start seriously learning to speak Italian. She recommended that I begin with learning the fifty to one hundred most important Italian verbs. She explained that learning these verbs would create both a base of understanding and a framework to slowly fill in over time for me.

She told me that if I could master one hundred verbs, I would be able to understand about half of what people said in Italian.

I immediately purchased a book titled *The 100 Most Important Italian Verbs*, along with a new leather-bound one-hundred-page blank journal which I titled "*Italian 2015*" in black ink. It was July of 2015, the fire inside of me was burning strong, and I felt highly motivated. My goal was to tackle one new verb; create an individual page in the journal for each verb; write them out in present, past, and future forms, singular and plural; and then create a few basic sentences (with the help of Google Translate) incorporating that particular verb each day. I felt writing the verb, seeing the verb written, then speaking the verb in a meaningful sentence would best help me learn.

Honestly, this exercise was kind of fun. Each day, I would sit at the desk in my home office for about forty-five minutes and work on the new verb of the day. I also made it a habit of reviewing the previous day's verb. On Sundays, I would spend maybe an hour just reviewing the past week's six new verbs, creating a few new sentences for each verb, looking for ways to combine some of the verbs in the same sentences, thinking about practical things I could link that verb to, and testing ways to improve my memory and association skills.

This first phase, which could be called the hundred verb phase, lasted to mid-November of 2015. My journal was full, and I spent the next few weeks on reviewing the verbs daily, usually practicing five verbs per day during my nearly hour-long lessons.

Phase two began Christmas week of 2015, as we returned to Italy for a three-week multi-city vacation. We landed in Rome, spent time in Assisi, Florence, again, Bologna, Pisa, then finished up with a solid week in Rome before returning home in mid-January. I was better prepared for this second trip. I had with me my new 2016 leather bound journal—a fatter one hundred and fifty pages now—where I had already transferred the 2015 'one hundred verbs, but my new format was a verb front and back of each page, so I had lots of room to add new verbs, and I reserved the last fifty pages for phrases that I planned on learning, beginning with this trip. I decided to alphabetize the verbs figuring it would make them easier to remember and quicker to go back and find.

I continued building the new 2016 journal every day for the next few months with the help of a new study book *The 250 Most Important Italian Verbs.* With each verb, I added the infinitive and a few other tense forms. By April of 2016, my new journal was full, so I purchased a new even larger leather-bound journal, named it *Italiano* 2016 #2, spent two weeks transferring all the two hundred and fifty previous journals verbs, but leaving lots of room for new verbs in each letter section. In May of 2016, we returned to Italy, this time mainly Rome, Ferrara, and Parma. Only fifteen days, but my learning agenda was full!

Chapter 18: The Learning Grows

Now about one year into the language journey, I felt my knowledge level had climbed from beginner to low-intermediate based upon feedback I was receiving from various workbook lessons, app tests, and interactions with native speakers.

It was at this point that I discovered and joined an Italian conversation group that met once per week at a local Italian restaurant. The group leader was the restaurant owner, originally from Naples, and a dozen of us would sit around one big table for about two hours, drink wine, eat a light meal, and speak only in Italian. Some members of the group were advanced, others just beginning, and some in the low to middle range like me. This conversation group was a really nice way for me to test out some of the content I had been so diligently learning. I enjoyed the weekly meetings and attended regularly for about nine months. Of course, during this period, I kept up my daily verb work, mixed in some new language apps, began watching Italian movies and TV series, and while driving, always has some Italian-language-learning CD playing on the stereo. This conversation group was a really good way for me to bring content and context together in a casual, low-pressure atmosphere. I would highly recommend it for anyone in this stage of language learning.

During this period of year two, I was fortunate enough to return to Italy once again in October of 2016 for two weeks of traveling mostly around the north, from Milano to

Verona to Venezia and Bologna. My 2016 journal #2 was by my side, as usual, being filled with more new words and phrases as they appeared. I forced myself to speak to as many people who were willing to speak with me in Italian. I knew my skills were not where they needed to be, but I tried to converse just the same. Maybe a bit embarrassing, but I pushed and tried and endured to certain funny looks that came my way in most of these awkward conversations.

Returning to Florida in November, I was filled with excitement and enthusiasm regarding my next few months of learning. I had fallen in love with Italian movies, watching them on TV and in theaters in Italy. They were so different from American films. Italian movies are light on shooting, car chases, special effects, but heavy on the drama, the story, the exaggerated emotions, and the devotion to Mama and old people in general. They tell a story, usually one of endurance, rarely have a happy ending, but suck you in deeply. And now, I was able to understand maybe half the dialogue, while able to figure out the other half with hand gestures, tears, and other typical Italian body language. I purchased a new DVD every week to watch. Some were so amazing I watched them multiple times! I also kept up the daily verb and app and workbook studies, pushing it to about an hour each day. I also mixed in some books like *Italian Short Stories for Beginners and Intermediates*.

Day in, day out, I continued to grind on. The fog was lifting, a little bit. I was able to understand more, speak more. Not a lot, but more than before. When in the presence of native speakers, talking amongst themselves, I was still unsteady and unsure. This was a little discouraging. I had probably committed over a thousand hours of studying at this point and wished I was farther along in my understanding level.

Another trip back to Italy, in March of 2017, then another that same summer, some new cities, some small towns, some new friends, a business opportunity in Rome (which continues to this day), more practicing, studying, movies, short stories, regular WhatsApp messaging and video calls with my business partner in Rome. This all bled into 2018, when I returned again to Rome in April.

Chapter 19: The Fog Starts Lifting

As I approached year four of my Italian language journey, I created a list titled "Going to the next level in Italian." My recollection at this point, the spring of 2018, was that I needed a big push to get me to the finish line. I was still enjoying the movies, the weekly back and forth with my man in Rome, but I was feeling a bit stuck, frustrated, and reviewing verb charts and journal notes and the same language apps over and over was beginning to get boring. That began to cause anxiety feelings that I may lose interest and abandon this already long voyage, similar to what happened in my quest to speak Spanish. Having recently returned from a nearly month-long visit in Rome and cities nearby Rome, having been really immersed in the language for four straight weeks, I was not happy with the level of my speaking and understanding skills. I could understand some things, say some things, but so much of this language was still a mystery for me. So by doing a pile of research, reading, inquiring, etc., I developed this "Going to the Next Level" list as a new roadmap for learning and a kickstart that I needed to keep pressing forward toward my goal of fluency. The list included ten learning strategies and began with the phrase "I will know victory when I'm able to freely understand and communicate in Italian. I will accept that I will never know every word and phrase and it doesn't matter. "

The ten main strategic points are the following:

- Immersion in native materials (listening and reading with *no* subtitles in English. Mostly podcasts, radio, TV, YouTube videos, vlogs, movies, books—stick to fun and interesting—no boring stuff.

- Increase from my current one hour/day language study to two hours/day.

- Boost my motivation by making connections between the study material and what I see and hear during native material immersion.

- Use the power of context—new words and phrases I really care about (like food) or must use to communicate (for travel).

- Watch episodes of *"Ted Talks Italiano"* on YouTube.

- Study with maximum focus and attention.

- Buy an Italian-language cookbook and use it to learn some new dishes.

- Emphasize listening more over reading.

- Buy and read an interesting and fun book written in Italian—don't stop when unsure—highlight word or phrase and revisit/translate at end of chapter.

- Spend one night per week binge watching fun Italian language movies or TV series.

Looking back, I spent the next nearly year quickly glancing at this list each morning (it was taped to the side of my computer tower), and following its strategies daily, different ones on different days, as I felt like doing. I can credit this list with giving me the lifeline, the motivation, the game plan, that I needed at that moment. It worked well enough to bridge me into year five and beyond. It worked also in the sense that it was through some of these new strategies that enabled me to up my game, get even more serious about the language learning, and boost my confidence to a level where I was beginning to feel comfortable speaking and listening to Italian. It was now in my blood, part of my daily routine, a habit I could not break. It was in this year, year four, that I knew that I was going to succeed. There was absolutely no chance I would quit or fail or come up short. I could smell it, taste it- I was getting close and felt certain that nothing was going to stop me now. My investment was huge and it had to pay off! This was also the point that I realized that over my entire life, I had never made such a sustained effort to learn something new anywhere near this magnitude. I had worked harder, and longer, towards this goal than anything else in my entire life.

So back to the summer of 2018 and the start of my so-called "next level" phase of the language journey. If I had to rate my Italian language skill level at that point, zero being where I began in the summer of 2015, now toward the end of 2020 being an 8.5, I was somewhere between a four and a five, probably closer to the four. A respectable move, but I was not there…yet. This "next level" plan was good, I had to fine tune it several times as 2018 turned into 2019, we took another Italy trip in November of 2018, a little more confidence and skill. By early 2019, following just under four years of diligent study, it was starting to come together.

The dots were beginning to connect. The fog that was "what did he say?" or "what does that mean?" was lifting. I could watch an Italian movie without subtitles, and as long as I was really focused on the dialogue, I was now able to understand more than half of everything being said. Thus, I was able to understand what was happening in the movie! Same with listening to Italian music, or Italian news shows. I could understand! Not every word, but enough to know what is going on. It felt like real progress, finally. Could I consider myself quasi fluent?

Chapter 20: Close but No Cigar

But…not just yet. Maybe I couldn't realize it, but all of my new "understanding" was in the warm, safe bubble of my house, my car- just me—no other real people. I found this out soon enough, in the early spring of 2019, as I spent just over two weeks in Rome and points south of Rome, in close company with some friends and my business partner who lived in a small city just south of Rome. During a three-day stay in this small city, surrounded by only Italian speakers, spending all of my time with them, I became aware of just how far away from fluency I really was. I discovered that when I was put on the spot to speak, to reply to something, to request a specific thing, from a "real" person who spoke no English, that I would still kind of freeze up, be unable to find the correct Italian words, and default in frustration to hand gestures peppered with a few Italian words. Although disappointing, on my very last night with my friends, before returning to Florida, we had what turned out to be maybe the greatest meal of my life, certainly the largest and longest. In Italian, they call it a *cenone* (big dinner).

Chapter 21: The Last Supper

The big meal (a small detour with an important discovery):

It happened in a town called *Artena* at a restaurant that is a shrine to Mussolini called *Ristorante Il Federale*. My friend, as it became clear, is a big shot in that area and a good friend of this restaurant owner. I share this experience with you for two reasons: first, after drinking copious amounts of wine and grappa over many, many hours, and sitting at a private table with ten men and women who spoke nothing but Italian with me being the guest of honor (or curiosity), there came a point when I was conversing clearly and confidently in Italian, as I was able to view videos the following day as proof. Maybe I was relaxed enough, comfortable enough, and all that verbiage just started flowing like lava out of Mount Vesuvius. And second, for anyone who appreciates great food and drink, this meal could be compared to stopping by your neighborhood pub for a beer and some jukebox music, and all of a sudden, the Rolling Stones walk in, get up on the bar, Keith and Ron plug in their guitars, Mick picks up the mic, and they proceed to play their greatest hits for the next seven hours. This was the Federal greatest dining experience of my life, bar none. It started as a "late lunch" or *"un po pranzo"* at about two pm. We were the only guests in this old, museum-like building, on a dark, stormy, rain-soaked afternoon. It began with the ten of us sitting around a large table, about six waitstaff and the chef giving us their full attention. Our table opened to a large, covered outdoor terrace, overlooking mountains and fierce weather.

There were no menus. The antipasti (appetizers) just started coming, a new one about every ten minutes or so, each accompanied by a new wine. Meats, cheeses, vegetables—easily eight separate courses and eight separate wines. My pants were starting to feel tight. A small pause, and then la pasta, a flurry of different pasta dishes in different sauces, each accompanied by its own wine, I counted six pasta courses, each better and richer than the next.

It was now approaching five pm, I opened my belt and the top button on my pants, had eaten enough in the past three hours to last me a week, drank countless glasses of some incredible wines, was speaking Italian (almost) like a native, and at this point had no idea that we were barely into halftime! Another small pause, we wobbled onto the outdoor covered patio, had more wine, joked about the storm and the beauty of the mountain view we had, sat back down at the table, and a new train started pulling into the station. *I Primi*. The meats. So much meat, so many different cuts and types and seasonings, and, of course, each new meat came with a new wine! For the next ninety minutes or so, with fork and knife in hand, we devoured many pounds of carne until we all seemed to hit the wall. This is when my second pants button opened, and I was getting dizzy from having just eaten enough food to keep a town going for a month.

The storm was raging outside, it was dark, and nearing seven pm when the meat plates were all cleared. Then, like defying gravity, came the salads. It seems Italians eat their salads not before, but after the main courses. Something about digestion? To be honest, the salads were kind of easy. Some plates of lettuce, tomatoes, a little fruit, and some Prosecco wine. It was like stepping over a puddle after having swum the English Channel. And then, like a paddle shock to the heart, espresso and grappa appeared! I had two or three espresso, a grappa, and then the desserts began: cheesecake, rum cake, cannoli, fruits, creams, more coffee, and more grappa. We finished the meal at nine pm, all outside on the patio, with a final toast, a salute! To life, to health, to friends. We hugged, we kissed, we limped back to our vehicles. This was a seven-hour food and wine marathon—something I had never experienced or had even known existed. Apparently, it was a local custom. Back to my hotel. Pass out in a food coma. Wake up in the morning and fly home to Florida. I'm just lucky Alitalia didn't charge me for the "extra weight" on the return flight.

Chapter 22: A Lightbulb Goes Off

And it was during this return flight that I had the chance to review pics and vids of the previous night's banquet and see and listen to myself speaking Italian pretty well—not perfect but understandable—during this long, relaxed, friendly meal. And this is where I recognized that my biggest hurdle at this point in my language learning journey was not my knowledge content, but rather my confidence to speak when around native speakers. It occurred to me that I was putting too much pressure on myself to speak "perfect" Italian when around Italians when in fact that is not necessary in order to communicate well. So, I made a few notes in my journal, reminding myself that as I continue my learning journey that I will make a conscious effort to just speak, even if it's not a grammatically perfect word or sentence. Simply relax and let the words flow. Don't think so much and remember that I don't have to impress anyone. If I make a few mistakes, then so what!

Back home in Florida, April 2019:

Before even catching up on some pressing work-related issues, I recalled the urgency that I felt with regard to my language journey, specifically how I was going to move ahead with my recently discovered self-knowledge? Knowing myself, I needed a plan, to write it out, look it over, edit it for a few days, then post it near my desk and run with it. That's exactly what I did over the first week back. Well, actually, I also booked my next trip back to Rome, set for September, just a day on the return home! I needed to go back, keep it moving. I was beginning to smell the faint scent of victory. I knew I was closing in on it. Not quite there yet but getting closer.

Chapter 23: Next Level Move

The plan:

Having about five months to prepare for the next trip and in possession of new self-knowledge, I created a twenty-week language learning agenda that required ninety minutes of practice per day, each day requiring a minimum of ten minutes verb review, ten minutes short story reading, thirty minutes of Duolingo app work(I had finished the entire app from beginning to end already, and was beginning my second lap by mid-summer), ten minutes of phone conversation with either my business partner or friend Marianna, advanced conversation CDs playing nonstop in my daily driver vehicle, and enjoying some pieces of Italian language movies or TV series in the evening. The goal now was to return to Rome in September as a fluent native speaker. In my mind, it felt not only possible but probable. Was I in for a surprise!

Back in Rome September 2019:

Immediately upon landing at Fiumicino Airport, I could feel the extra muscle that had grown from all the hard studying and practicing over the past months. I had been diligent, missed maybe a day or two days max, and far exceeded my study times on many other days. My reading and writing and comprehension felt strong, I felt confident, I thought I was "there." Sorry, wrong, not ready for prime time yet.

As I re-engaged with some friends and business associates, I was hesitant, at a loss for words, and definitely not fluent. I was able to "squeeze" by with lots of gestures and facial expressions, but my speaking ability was still lacking. But how could this be? In my mind, I thought that I had crossed the finish line. But in reality, there was still a long way to go. Anyway, I thoroughly enjoyed the trip, the great food, wine, art, walking, architecture, and those beautiful Italian high-speed trains—*I Frecci*. In my hotel room each night before retiring, I continued my daily Duolingo app lessons and worked on a travelogue in Italian only.

Returning home to Florida in early October, I felt happy, content, but a little unfulfilled in my language journey. Something was missing, and I needed to figure out what it was exactly. I was approaching four and a half years of serious, committed, focused learning and studying and practicing of the Italian language, and when honestly self-reflecting on my proficiency could not declare fluency! I recall the thought crossing my mind that I had spent more time than getting a college degree, with no summers or vacations off, on just one single subject, Italian, and was still coming up short. So, what was the answer?

Chapter 24: Conquering Self-Doubt

Was it possible that at my age I was incapable of becoming fluent in a second language? Was I too old? Was my brain too fossilized? Did I not want it bad enough? Was I not smart enough? (PS I was a college dropout.) Was this some silly vanity project that didn't deserve a happy ending?

So, I went back to the Ben Franklin problem solving method, sat at my desk, alone, with a sheet of blank paper, and began writing possible solutions to this problem. The one that made the most sense involved how I was going about the learning. My own learning processes were good but maybe not good enough. The question now was how to improve how I learn. I went online, searched books that explored how the mind absorbs information, and specifically how to best absorb a new language. After hours of book research, I came across one that seemed to fit my dilemma best.

Once the book arrived, I read it immediately. Basically, over the past four plus years, I had done many of the right things. Learning the verbs, the tenses, the conjugations, the reading, the movies, the apps. Good stuff, stuff anyone would have to do. But I discovered that I had also been hurting myself with English subtitles, translation apps, and a few other things. This book explained that in order to rise to the level of fluency, what was required was total immersion with no English to distract or disrupt the lessons (be they movies or books or CD's or music, or apps) It was now mid-October 2019, and time for a reset and a restart. I booked a New Year's Eve day flight to Rome with my family (nine of us—oh yes), planned the next few months of immersion lessons, and hit the books!

Now not so focused on perfection, but more on absorbing larger quantities of untranslated, authentic, native-spoken content for a minimum of ninety minutes per day every day until the New Year's trip. This was my main focus for the next ten weeks. And honestly it was a nice change from my past studying. I put away the verb charts, the translation workbooks, the half English half Italian CDs and really let it rip with the all-Italian native speaking and reading content. I would spend time each day bouncing around various Italian language vlogs, Ted Talks in Italian, switched to watching only Italian movies with no subtitles, and started reading real books written in Italian, books that were interesting and fun. Looking back to that ten-week period closing out 2019, each day I felt more and more comfortable with this immersion content, ok with the reality that although I could not understand every word said, I was able to understand the majority of words and the details of the conversations. I was starting to recognize word patterns—certain words and phrases used more frequently than most—and focused on those more. Words like what, when, who, where, how when connected to the main verbs, have, do, must, want, speak, move. This is the point where the 'fog" really began to lift. The words, the sentences, they all started to come into focus, clearly, and really for the first time.

Once again, I felt good, confident, and enthusiastic about moving forward in my language journey. I think I could describe best how I felt at this point. It was like I had all this learned data (verbs, tenses, conjugations, phrases, masculine and feminine) bottled up tightly in my brain, but when I needed to use it, there was a sort of bottleneck in my mouth that wouldn't allow the saved data to flow out freely. It was like three lanes of traffic being squeezed into one lane. But by trying this new immersion learning, the bottleneck was opening, the lanes of traffic were widening, and it was at this point that it started flowing more naturally, more confidently, more easily.

Chapter 25: Torniamo a Roma!

New Year's Day 2020:

We were all in Rome in Vatican Square, waiting for the Pope to step out on his balcony and bless the massive crowd of over a hundred thousand people. We arrived early and positioned ourselves well.

The sun was shining, the wind was blowing, it was cold, but it was beautiful. Dozens of small weddings were going on around us. Music and flowers and champagne corks were popping. The air was crisp and clean and smelled so good! My 1-year-old grandson is on my shoulders. He is bundled up and smiling from ear to ear. Our Airbnb was in *Trastevere*, only a ten-minute walk from *il Vaticano*. We had stopped for some cappuccinos and pastries on the way. We required nutrition and warmth for the cobblestone hike! No one does coffee and pastries better than the Romans!

Papa Francesco stepped out on the papal balcony, spoke in clear and strong Italian for about fifteen minutes, gave his blessing, and disappeared back inside. I can describe this experience as both spiritual (seeing the Pope so close) and rewarding (being able to understand what he said) The payoff from four and a half years of studying, practicing, pushing forward. It was finally starting to unfold!

We spent the next few weeks together in Rome, eating, drinking, walking, exploring, and enjoying. I used every opportunity that presented itself to use my new best friend, the Italian language. I was like a child with a new toy! I would sit down at a table with a bunch of old Italian guys playing cards and drinking wine, introduce myself, and spend the next few hours in the game. I would spend a half hour in a clothing store discussing with the salesperson which jacket would be better to buy. I would go to the local outdoor market and spend an hour talking to different vendors about where they buy their cheese from or where the fish come from, how much for this, how much for that. Granted, neither my comprehension nor my speaking was perfect or even really good, but they were good enough (*abbastanza bene*) for me to get by (*mi lo cavo*) and for me to understand and be understood. My goal was never, and never will be, to become a Nobel prize winner in Italian language. The goal was to comprehend and speak, and now I was doing just that.

Chapter 26- *"The Obstacle Is the Way"*

Back in Florida January-February 2020—the home stretch (and the beginning of the COVID nightmare):

Following a brief recovery from the big holiday trip (just a few days) and putting out some fires at work, it was time, once again, to plan the next course of study and tactics. We were still in the pre-COVID-19 period, so this soon to be nightmare was not factored into the game plan.

Sitting at my desk, reflecting on the sacrifices and effort I had made over the past four and a half years, plus the most recent semi- fluency breakthrough I experienced in Italy and wanting to get to an even better level of understanding in speaking Italian, my focus shifted to several fronts: First, I did not want to lose touch with all the verbs and tenses and conjugations. Second, I felt a need to smooth out the rough edges that I was still struggling with, especially when speaking. Third, and this may sound weird, but I really missed my daily Duolingo app lessons. And finally, since it was obvious that the ten-week immersion prior to the new year had really worked, I felt it important to continue and even expand, as possible.

As February 2020 became March became April, I had returned to my reliable and predictable study habits with a twist. Let me explain.

Chapter 27: Back to basics

To reinforce and stay conscious with all the verbs and tenses and conjugations that I had been plowing through like a giant cornfield for years, I pulled out an old friend *The 2,000 Most Important Italian Words and Phrases* workbook. This book I had already gone through one time forward with highlighting and notes, one time backward with more highlights and notes, and a third time while taking notes onto a separate journal. For this, the fourth go around, I went from end to beginning, covering fifty words/phrases per night, every night for forty straight nights. About an hour each session right after dinner. But this time, I would take the word or phrase and create my own new phrase to incorporate it into. So, I had to think hard and be creative to create the alternate phrases. When this was done, I devoted another forty days in a fifty phrase per session review of the new phrases, which took only about thirty minutes to accomplish per night. This eighty-day-long exercise helped to cement, hopefully permanently into my brain, these core verbs and phrases. My guess is about eighty percent instant recall success, the other twenty percent is buried deep but can be recalled with a little stall time or a quick *dizionario* look-up.

To address some of my rough edges, particularly when speaking, I made up a game with myself. I've already told you that I am a builder. A sizable part of every workday involves driving from one job site to the next. I'm usually alone in my vehicle for two to three hours each day. Maybe an hour of that driving time is spent on phone calls, but that leaves plenty of time to play my game. It's simple, corny, maybe geeky. I assess my surroundings as I drive and in the privacy of my vehicle describe what I see only in Italian. This usually evolves into whole "self-conversations"—just me talking to myself about the weather, the pedestrians, the other drivers, or anything that comes into view and looks interesting. After a while, I'm not just speaking in Italian, I'm also thinking in Italian. And going one step further, I now find myself having Italian conversations with myself each morning in the shower. A few years ago, I had a steam machine installed for my shower, and each morning I usually take a ten-to-twelve-minute steam before showering. All these low pressure, safe, thoughtful self-conversations have allowed me to increase my Italian speaking skills and improve my confidence speaking with native speakers. My kids think I'm annoying when they overhear me speak, but so what! I continue to move forward, get better, and be proud of it!

I also rekindled my daily love affair with the Duolingo app. Although I had previously finished the entire app nearly two years before, then ventured back to it last year for a few months of daily review, it had always been the most fun way for me to practice. There was just something about competing with thousands of other language learners on a daily basis. With maybe thirty minutes of total practice time spread out during the day, I would usually rank in the top twenty, sometimes even the top ten, and once finished a weekly competition at number two! And there was another aspect of this app that grabbed me hard and wouldn't let me go- it was always available on my phone which would allow me to use any downtime during my day or evening, as long as I wasn't driving, to squeeze out a ten-minute lesson and be more productive. I had developed an early morning habit of first coffee and then a ten-minute Duolingo lesson. And during the workday or even an off day, I would always do one or two lessons when alone and the time was right. Then at night, always before retiring to sleep, one last lesson, usually in bed, imprinting just a little more Italian language into my mind before I doze off. This whole Duolingo lesson process gave me a warm feeling of maximum accomplishment each day- although just a piece of the whole learning puzzle. It's how I started each day and ended each day. It had become a habit in my life that I really liked.

In continuance of the immersion portion of my learning journey, I restarted the habit of watching some daily Italian only (no subtitles) movies and TV series, of which there is tons of free content on Netflix and Amazon Prime. This would typically last about thirty minutes each evening or sometimes I could even do it on my phone during the workday, in the privacy of my office, as time and work obligations permitted. With the Internet, with Wi-Fi, there are really no limits anymore. And to round out the daily immersion learning (at least thirty to forty-five minutes), I returned to the *Gazzetta di Parma* app, and spend fifteen minutes somewhere during the day reading articles, restaurant reviews, weather forecasts, etc., all in Italian with no translations.

So basically, this phase of the language journey could be called the four-legged stool: verbs and tenses, smooth out rough edges, Duolingo app, and more immersion. As February and March turned into April, I would estimate my daily total study time at two hours. And then COVID and the lockdown and lots of extra free time all of a sudden. Great! I love free time because it gives me more time to work on myself. I say this because I truly believe it.

Chapter 28: Beyond Language

Learning this new language is only part of my self-growth. I work hard each day, as a practicing Stoic, trying to improve my thoughts, my actions, my outcomes. I've been a practicing Stoic for many years now, spend about fifteen minutes each morning in my Stoic training, but that's another story, another book. I also try to stay in good physical shape, which requires a combination of gym work and running totaling forty-five minutes five days per week. Plus, I have a bunch of kids and a wife and they all need something from me every day. If you're thinking "where does this guy get all this time" for studying, self-improvement, working out, family obligations, etc., the answer is simple.

First of all, I'm very organized in most of the things that I do. This allows me to get the most done in the least amount of time. I am a creature of habit and have developed, over decades, quite good habits. I have worked very hard to identify and eliminate any of my old bad habits. The net result of my good organizational skills, my good daily habits, my lack of bad habits, and my self-discipline have as a byproduct allowed my construction business to flourish beyond my wildest dreams. The business has reached a point that it runs, almost on autopilot and generates more money than we need to live a fabulous life. I have cultivated, over the last fifteen or so years, a group of young, honest, reliable, and capable people that do ninety percent or more of the work that I used to do. Although I am still the owner and "face" of the company, my daily work requirements require typically no more than three or four hours. That's it, really. A few drive-bys on the job sites, a meeting here and there, a trip to the bank to deposit checks, and writing checks when needed. I have been lucky enough and worked hard and smart enough, over the years to have developed a devoted following in a very exclusive, high-end sector of the home building market in Palm Beach, Florida.

Chapter 29: Lockdown

Back to April 2020:

We are in almost full lockdown due to the COVID-19. That means, among other things, even more free time.

Free time to do more family stuff.

Free time to get smarter, stronger, better. Let's focus on the smarter, stronger, better. I committed to increase my daily Italian study time by fifty percent, or to about three hours each day. My thought was that if I could sustain this increased study level for the next three or four months, that the results would speak for themselves and push me up a notch higher. I could expand the four-legged stool and even mix in a fifth aspect. I purchased a new Alfa Romeo with advanced electronics and defaulted all the voice commands (phone, directions, vehicle modes) to Italian, while simultaneously defaulting my iPhone also to Italian only. These two audio mediums, which are with me most of the day, bombard me with even more Italian language and force me to speak and navigate in Italian more than ever.

Chapter 30: The Light at the End of the Tunnel Is Now Visible

August and September 2020:

It's been a busy and intense summer! Tons of new construction projects and lots of daily work on the five-legged stool. Navigating life and work during the COVID-19 crisis, which continues to rage throughout the USA, especially Florida, it's been like an episode of the *Twilight Zone*. I could say that the past six months have been the most productive and rewarding ever in both business and language learning. My family and I are all lucky and blessed. No one has been infected with the virus, and for some strange reason the segment of the construction industry where I focus has been absolutely on fire and continues to expand flourish.

However, it is clear that many, many people—those who work (or worked) in the restaurant business, the hotel business, retail businesses, entertainment businesses, or anything related to travel and tourism—these people are hurting. They are living mainly off government subsidies, waiting on food lines, and uncertain about their futures and the futures of their children. It is sad to see this unfolding on a daily basis in such a rich country and in such a rich area of the country.

On top of the pandemic, another crisis rages in parallel, the political war that is leading up to a major election on the first Tuesday of November. It's the Biden vs Trump main event! It has our country more divided than it's been in many years, along economic lines, racial lines, party lines, religious lines, state lines. It's unfolding like a soap opera with almost daily scandals uncovered, plot twists, and dishonesty piled a mile high. It's ugly and in our face's day and night. The Republicans have cast themselves as the party of God, the protector of the status quo, the wall standing between law and order versus chaos and rioting, the party of "real" Americans versus communists/socialists/America haters, and their leader is a five-time bankrupt carnival barker who wouldn't know the truth if it sat on his face and wiggled! The Democrats portray themselves as the party of inclusion, of acceptance, of tolerance, of empathy- and are led by a nearly 80-year-old career politician who, although he seems like a nice guy, may not be up to the challenge of the job. So, two choices, neither really good. I'm amazed that our beautiful, strong, wealthy, and democratic country could not offer better choices for the top job, someone younger with vision, with fire and the gravitas to be a president that most Americans could be proud of.

Enough about work, about COVID, about politics. Let's get back to the nuts and bolts of language learning, ok? Let's look closer at the five-legged stool, which I worked daily and diligently through November.

The five-legged stool final push:

1- As mentioned already, I leaned back into the Duolingo app. Kind of like the feeling of a soft, warm blanket. This app, now updated with dozens of new lessons, plus all the older lessons, was how I started my day, ended my day, and filled in about thirty minutes of practice during the day. Words and phrases that I had learned three years ago reviewed again last year and now are revisiting for a third time are familiar at a rate above eighty percent, maybe close to ninety percent. For the handful of words and phrases that are still elusive, or semi-forgotten, I take a moment to stop the lesson, switch over to the *dizionario* app, and look it up. I'll see it, speak it, write it down, and return to the lesson. Then at the very end, I do a final review of the tough ones. This seems to work well. I think because it's old material that I learned already, and the "bones" of the meaning are embedded deep inside my head already. To bring them back to life requires a simple refresh. My guess would be that with this third push on Duolingo I'm at or above ninety-five percent comprehension after the final reviews.

I could say this with confidence because I'm scoring one hundred percent on about every third lesson and in the low to mid-nineties on the rest. It's fun, it's competitive, it's rewarding, and it's testing my brain for about forty-five minutes every day. I plan to continue until at least year end 2020.

2- With regards to the immersion learning portion of this summer/fall/ early-winter time period, my goal was to find new Italian language movies and TV series on Amazon Prime, which carries lots of Italian content. As a Prime member, most of it streams instantly to my iPhone or laptop and is absolutely free. So, I find myself watching about seven hours of strictly Italian language shows with no subtitles on a weekly basis. I've learned that when the actors are speaking really fast or injecting some regional dialect, as long as I really focus hard, watch the movements and expressions and reactions, I'm able to understand the majority of the dialogue. When they are speaking slowly or even at normal pace, my comprehension rate is at ninety percent plus.

In addition, the daily *Gazzetta di Parma* reviews continue, the usual fifteen or so minutes, one or two local stories, mostly about crime, immigration, or the COVID cases still lingering. I do enjoy an occasional story on local Parma politics, especially when it concerns the Mayor (sindaco) of Parma. We are friends of his, wish him well, and cringe at some of the stories and allegations that are thrown his way almost weekly. Italian politics is very personal, very in your face. Cities in the north, like Parma, were hit especially hard during the pandemic. In addition, there has been a significant rise in immigration over the past few years, mostly from Africa and the Middle East where the migrants who land in the south wind up moving north in search of jobs. But unfortunately, the jobs are not there, either. This creates a difficult situation for the residents, the officials, and the immigrants. Most of them are young men, and without job opportunities, it places an unwanted burden on the residents, increases crime dramatically, and is a real hot-button issue throughout the peninsula with no clear solutions. It has also given rise to a far-right political movement, as well as giving opportunities to existing mafiosi to play both sides of the issue in their own favor.

Hopefully this crisis will have a happy ending in the near future.

3- In continuing the self-conversations leg while driving and even sometimes showering, this slightly weird but effective language-learning technique which I simply dreamed up earlier in the year forged forward each day. Depending on how much driving, how many phone calls, how much mental focus was needed to carry out my construction work requirements on that particular day, I have been averaging twenty to thirty minutes daily. The goal is to not just spew Italian words and phrases as I whip around town in the Alfa Romeo, but by doing this I'm actually thinking in Italian, and that is molding my consciousness more toward fluency in this new language. Since I'm by myself, there is no pressure to speak perfectly, I can make mistakes with no audience to chastise or correct me. It's a completely relaxed atmosphere, as well as being kind of fun to do. And it gets more fun the better I get at speaking!

4-Advancing the verbs and tenses learning leg, this required another trip down memory lane. I pulled out my 2019 Verbs and Phrases leather-bound journal, which was my fifth and final version of these self-created, alphabetical, now at three different verbs per page with the final fifty pages a compilation of what I had considered the most commonly used and useful Italian phrases, totaling approximately three hundred and fifty. The verb section was now just over five hundred verbs, listed alphabetically, each with a past, present, future, and action example, including one sentence showcasing that verb. This journal had travelled with me to

Rome for the New Year's trip, had some sauce and wine stains on several pages, a few primitive drawings of the Ponte Sisto (a twelve-hundred-year-old pedestrian bridge we crossed several times per day), a sketch of the fountain, designed by Bernini, in front of the Chiesa di Santa Maria, a stone's throw from our rented Villa in Trastevere, a quick drawing of the Giordano Bruno statue, standing above the Campo Fiori market and memorializing a Catholic Priest who was burned at the stake on that very spot in the year sixteen hundred, for the "crime" of actually believing and repeating some of Galileo's theories, a rough, and penciled drawing of the Scale Santa inside a seventeen-year-old church, this is a marble staircase that was transported from Jerusalem to Rome in the third century AD, steps that Jesus Christ has himself walked on, bled on, and healed on. So, this beautiful, red, soft leather-bound journal, tucked snuggly into my cross-body bag was not just part of a few incredible weeks bouncing around Rome, it held all of my current verb knowledge and the majority of my phrase understanding. So, flipping through the pages, now over six months later, I was able in some ways to re-live those beautiful weeks, feel like I was almost there, smell the smells, hear the sounds, taste the tastes, and vividly recall any notes I had jotted down, the sketches, the stains. The verbs were even more alive than they were before. They were like five hundred old friends, most of whose names I was able to remember and the ones that were still a bit unclear at first glance, most came back to me pretty quickly. A handful I had to look up the meaning for, but maybe only about ten. As I glanced through this journal, which I kept on my desk in an unavoidable spot, maybe fifteen minutes each day, it did not feel like studying, or work. Instead, it felt more like I was just bumping into lots of old friends, remembering their names, their nicknames, and having fun. I connected the journal to the holiday trip. Each time it was in my hands, I felt somewhat transported back to my favorite city, with my favorite people, eating my favorite foods, and enjoying my favorite pastimes and art. This was a strong, emotional connection, with very positive feelings, and it made the fifteen or so minutes of daily verb review fly by quicker than a set of pushups! It was actually enjoyable to reconnect with the verbs, the tenses, the conjugations, knowing I had let them slip a bit over the past year, and rediscovering them in a way that was almost a vacation in itself!

5- Finally, with regard to smoothing out some rough edges, this required a small step back, some critical and honest self-analysis, identifying any weak or rough areas in my Italian comprehension and speaking abilities, and then to focus on them. The goal was to bring them to the surface, make a short list of them, assign to each of them a practical remedy, and get to work fixing them. I found that I would still "freeze" like a deer in the headlights when Italian was spoken at me fast and direct, my brain scanning for the "perfect" response. So, I learned about a dozen "filler/staller" words or phrases, that sounded native, but it gave me a few seconds to process the question and respond better. Filler/staller words like "well, you know," "sometimes," "let me think for a second," etc.

Another weak spot was comprehension while watching Italian TV or films, especially when spoken quickly. To overcome this problem, I discovered that if I listened intently, with focus and concentration, I was able to understand the words and phrases much better.

Lastly, I detected weakness at times in conveying my response in Italian. I reminded myself of the unimportance of perfection and to stay calm and relaxed during the communication—then it would usually just flow out—and who cares about an occasional mispronunciation or grammar error? The important part is that I understand the speaker and get my point across accurately It's not about impressing other people with flawless language execution. It's about communicating successfully. That's the goal.

Chapter 31: Onward and upward!

As we approach the holidays and New Year's 2021, I continue my language lessons, although I've cut back on the daily time investment. My plan is to finish the year out, about six weeks to go, with just an hour per day devoted to Italian practice. It's split pretty evenly between the Duolingo app, the *Gazetta di Parma* reading, Italian movies and TV shows, and a short Whatsapp call with my friend in Rome. Then, during that week between Christmas and New Year's, a time when no economic work is competing with my learning and thinking, just as I've done for at least the last twenty-five years, use this downtime for two things: First, an honest and accurate review of the recently completed year. I always review my previous year's goal list and compare that list to what actually happened over the year. Some of the goals are personal, some are business, and some relate to self-growth. I actually give myself a score on each list item, then an overall score for the year. Although a bit premature, I have a strong feeling that the year 2020 will score very high. I already know that I have well surpassed my business and economic goals. Also, some of my self-growth goals, like my crossing the fluency line in Italian and my continued intense study and practice and acceptance of Stoicism. Some of the personal goals, related to family and friends, have generally worked out well but certainly leave lots of room for future improvement. The one thing that will fall short, way short, of my last year's goal was staying in and getting into even better physical shape. Since my teenage years, I've pretty consistently maintained a good balance of healthy eating, running, and weightlifting.

This has enabled me, at six feet one inch, to hover around two hundred pounds with a muscular upper body and pretty good abs. Unfortunately, I went into the wrong direction on this matter. Few of my pants and shirts fit properly, I've gained at least twenty pounds, and have been doing little physical exercise since early spring. These things are all mind over matter, and I think that I convinced myself that as a consequence of the COVID-19 lockdowns, coupled with my intense focus on learning and self-improvement, piled on top of the busiest and brightest economic work year in my life, I gave myself a "hall pass" on physical fitness for most of the year. Correction of this "aberration" will be on my new goals list for next year

And second, I create a new list of goals for the new year ahead. The goals that are still in progress may carry over from one year to the next. Sometimes priorities or circumstances change, and certain old goals are not so important and certain new goals come into focus.

This year annual goals list habit I have, which my Grandpa Joe taught me long ago, has helped me tremendously over the years to accomplish things I thought were impossible or improbable. The list is usually focused on a few priorities, split between family, friends, business, and self-growth. It's always in writing on a single sheet of heavy paper, split and drawn like a pie chart. I keep the list on my desk, but only where I can see it, no one else. It's my list, it belongs to my inner mind, and I view it as a challenge between my mind and my body. I feel that this list is so very personal, so important, such a big part of who I am and that it keeps me organized and focused.

I even make weekly lists—usually on Sunday evenings—that include the coming six days, Monday through Saturday, on a single piece of paper on a clipboard that sits beside me on my desks and my vehicles, always and all through the week. I've been doing this for over twenty years. It's a habit, and its part of my daily routine (except when on vacation or on Sundays) These weekly lists include the main work tasks of my week, some personal commitments, and a few notes regarding language learning, workouts, and Stoicism study. As each day moves forward and the list items are done, I scratch a line through the task and a checkmark at the end. This ritual gives me a sense of accomplishment and once all the day's items are scratched and checked, I know my day was productive and now it's over. It's a good feeling, one that allows me a little pre-sleep TV-watching, a steam, and then a good night's sleep. It protects me from procrastination, from forgetting anything important, and keeps me very organized. This weekly list helps me stay focused on the main goals and each day's essential tasks. It has developed my self-discipline, my self-knowledge, and has helped to thicken my skin against problems or distractions that pop up along the way.

Back to the annual list:

As the year progresses, I find myself crossing things off the list, things that have been accomplished or things that are no longer important. Sometimes I add a new goal or adjust an existing goal due to changing circumstances. The goals list gives me a lot of satisfaction from imagining things, writing them down, and making them become real. It's also taught me that I'm not all the way there yet with many things, but that's OK. The goals list reminds me every day that to create things, real and valuable things, requires effort, struggle and some pain. I know that as long as I have the strength to plan, learn, and create that I will continue moving forward and higher. I also learned that time spent alone, quietly, allows you to gain clarity and focus on the important things in your life, organize them, analyze them, prioritize them, and get them into motion.

I've already began to imagine how I want to frame the goal of Italian language learning into next year. The goal will be a higher and cleaner level of fluency. The tactics and techniques will probably be a mix of previous lessons and habits with some new methods mixed in to push a bit higher. I realize that to continue my learning journey, that my commitment must remain intense and focused.

Chapter 32: Conclusion and Success

As I mentioned early on, this is my first attempt at writing a book, so please excuse any grammatical, form, or style issues. Also, this book is skewed from an adult perspective and involves no school or formal classes. It is essentially a self-teaching guide to learn a second language as an adult. The main ingredients for success boil down to just a few things: possessing a strong motivation to learn, developing good daily study habits, allowing time and having patience, an open mind for different types of learning materials, and a genuine personal commitment to follow through and succeed. Planning your journey, executing your journey, and ultimately succeeding at becoming fluent in a second language will not be easy nor will it come quickly.

Learning a new language, especially as an adult, is similar to fighting a war. Like a war, there will be many small battles, fought day in and day out, gaining a little bit of ground at a time. Wars are fought over years, not days or weeks. Winning the war requires good strategies, good tactics, good discipline, and daily sacrifice. Unfortunately, there are no shortcuts. At least none that I could find. It's about putting in the work, every day, with passion, relentlessly, until you are finally there. The road is long and sometimes bumpy. So, you must develop better patience and endurance. Your brain may cry out for rest, for distraction, for help. So, you must resist taking the easy and more comfortable road. Your friends and family will begin to question you about the time you spend on your lessons and not with them. You must remind yourself of the prize that awaits you at the end and ignore their complaints. You may begin to get bored with your current study materials, which can lead to missed days and being easily distracted. You can prevent this by continually looking for new study content, expanding ways to increase your daily exposure to the language, and mix in fun things (especially travel) when possible. It helps to be creative, develop your own learning games, your own journals, your own collection of books and movies, some new friends that speak that language.

I strongly suggest start with a blank journal and fill that journal with the one hundred most important verbs of your new language. Devote a page to each of the one hundred verbs. On that page, write the verb in its full form (to be, to have, to see, etc.), then list it in its past, present and future tenses with all the conjugations (I, you, he, she, we, they, etc.) You will notice a pattern emerging with the tenses and conjugations, and, of course, there will be some important irregular verbs that require even more attention. Try including a sentence where that verb is used. You can also create a section, maybe the last fifty pages of the journal, in which you start compiling some commonly used words and phrases. Try to spend about thirty minutes per day building this beginning journal and include some time to review previous day's work. It helps to list the verbs alphabetically.

While you are working to create your first verb and phrase journal, download a beginner's level app, and try to devote fifteen minutes per day to it. If you find the app boring, move right onto another app until you are comfortable with one. Over my five-year journey, I went through about eight different apps and found most either boring or filled with errors. Only two—but especially Duolingo—were fun and I stuck with them. Also, as a possible third learning leg in this beginning phase, order a few very basic workbooks or short story books in that language, and try to devote fifteen minutes daily to this also. The goal now is to start getting familiar with some of the main verbs and phrases and develop a daily study routine that totals about forty-five minutes to an hour.

Then, after about two months, this first journal should be full. So now it's time to begin your second journal, this one a bit larger, say two hundred verbs, and more space again for commonly used words and phrases in the back. Begin this second journal by copying the first journal into it but leave an empty page between each verb. The empty page will soon be filled with your next batch of important verbs. Play around with different styles of how you create each verb page, something that sits well with you. This second journal will be one of many (maybe ten) to come and will form the backbone of the new language. You will find yourself referring back to it often, like your own homemade dictionary. You will continue to build it, customize it, and eventually master it! As you move on to the next journal, continue to copy the old content into the new, larger journal. Keep the old journals on your bookshelf if you want. You can look back on them with pride someday when you reach your goal of fluency.

So. as you move forward in your journey—the next journal, the next app, the next workbook or short story book—start increasing the levels of difficulty, and little by little begin adding more daily study time. Start mixing in movies, podcasts, TV shows in that language. At first, it will be very hard to understand anything but a few words but have faith! Patterns begin to develop, and a handful of words and phrases get used over and over. If it helps, write them down, look them up, and include them in your latest journal. If you have some travel opportunities, then test them out on real people. This is how you learn. If you mispronounce, or misspeak, the other person will probably just correct you! No big deal.

When you reach the end of year one, some of the conversational fog will begin to lift, and your verb knowledge should be pretty good. This will make you feel better, like all that daily studying is really working. It is, but if you are like me, there is still a long way to go. Fear not, this is not a sprint. It's a marathon. If you can accept that the language progress comes in small pieces over quite a long stretch of time, and that as long as you continue to push forward, each day, small step by small step, you will make it all the way.

Think about the early pioneers in pre-railroad America who crossed over three thousand miles in wagons, on horses, or walking, all the way from the East Coast to California. Imagine how long and painful that journey must have been when compared to your language journey, which is so much easier!

Some years ago, when I took running seriously (described earlier), as I began to feel exhaustion and pain set in during three- or four- or five-mile nightly runs, I would imagine a TV show that I had watched which documented an annual race across the Sahara Desert in Africa that was hundreds of miles long, took weeks to finish, and traversed very uncomfortable climates. When I put myself into the shoes of one of those competitors, I realized just how easy and short my own run was. This technique helped immensely.

As I crossed year two into year three, I realized exactly this. That it wasn't going to happen yet. I was not there yet. That this was going to be a long voyage, and to succeed was going to require a really serious continued commitment.

As mentioned much earlier, it really wasn't until crossing into year number five that understanding and speaking Italian became a reality for me. When I began this language journey in the summer of 2015, I did not have a specific study plan or a timetable. I did have a strong connection and motivation, I already had developed good study habits, and honestly felt nothing would stop me from becoming fluent. I guess, at that point, it was enough. Had I known it would take five years, I would have still moved ahead. Because looking back now, I have absolutely zero regrets regarding the time investment that was (and still is) required to become (and remain) fluent in a second language. when compared to the benefits, or the assets, that were acquired as a result. And you, too, will feel the same way, guaranteed!

Think about it for a moment—the time investment—an hour or two per day—which you can spread out or sprinkle into your normal routine—it's just not that big of a deal. A little less time spend on social media or watching TV or socializing and replacing that time with language learning materials instead. The payoff is that you are now bilingual. You have opened up new and exciting things that you didn't even know existed. You have developed really strong study and focus habits that have expanded and strengthened your mind, which can help you become better in other areas of your life. And the self-knowledge, the self-satisfaction that you set out on a long, difficult journey, where others doubted and criticized you, yet you made it.

Buona Fortuna (good luck).

Please, feel free to email me at:

jb@bellaconst.net

Ciao, Jeff

Made in the USA
Columbia, SC
08 March 2021